# SO THIS IS WHERE YOU WORK!

# *SO* THIS IS WHERE YOU WORK!

## A GUIDE TO UNCONVENTIONAL WORKING ENVIRONMENTS

### CHARLES A. FRACCHIA
### PHOTOGRAPHS BY MARK KAUFFMAN

A STUDIO BOOK · THE VIKING PRESS · NEW YORK

Text copyright by Charles A. Fracchia in all countries
of the International Copyright Union 1979
Photographs copyright by Mark Kauffman in all countries
of the International Copyright Union 1979
All rights reserved
First published in 1979
in simultaneous hard cover and paperback editions
by The Viking Press / A Studio Book and Penguin Books
625 Madison Avenue, New York, N.Y. 10022
Published simultaneously in Canada by
Penguin Books Canada Limited

Library of Congress Cataloging in Publication Data
Fracchia, Charles A. 1937–
  So this is where you work!
  (A Studio book)
  l. Buildings—United States—Remodeling for
other use. I.  Kauffman, Mark.  II.  Title.
NA2793.F7     725     78-27664
ISBN 0-670-65481-4

Printed in Japan

This book is dedicated to my parents, Charles B. and
Josephine Giacosa Fracchia, who, from my earliest years,
taught me the dignity and sacramental nature of work,
and whose constant and unqualified love has been the
mainstay of my life.

# Contents

## Introduction

**I**n the stage setting of Richard Wagner's opera *Die Meistersinger von Nürnberg* the closely situated houses in the medieval city are used both as places of business and as homes. All business—sales, manufacturing, design— and professional services were conducted on the ground floor, while the family, apprentices, and servants lived on the upper floors.

The Industrial Revolution and its aftermath were to destroy the intimate bond between a person's residence and his place of employment. The gospel of economic efficiency, coupled with the new technological demands of the industrial age, gained prominence over comfort and convenience. Labor became subject to the law of the most economically effective use of property rather than to human-scale considerations.

Thus during the nineteenth and twentieth centuries populations became concentrated in large cities; huge factory complexes—to which thousands of workers began to commute from their homes, often for hours each day— were constructed; and that twentieth-century phenomenon, the skyscraper, came into prominence—a modern Tower of Babel that has replaced biblical linguistic alienation with the physical and spiritual alienation of working within massive constructions of glass, steel, and concrete.

The trend to minimize the importance of the architectural and decorative aspects of working spaces rather than to fashion them into places where one takes pride in working, where one's individuality is taken into account, where there is sufficient access to natural light and air, did not die with the grimy, labyrinthine factories of the nineteenth and early twentieth centuries. The World Trade Center in New York, the John Hancock building in Chicago, and the Bank of America building in San Francisco, despite their plush interiors and imposing exteriors, can be just as antithetical to the human spirit as the earliest steel factory.

If a person lives in a large, modern apartment house, enclosed within the stucco walls and low ceilings of two or three tiny rooms; if he drives a car through snarled traffic, or takes a bus or train for miles to his place of work—an urban skyscraper or a vast factory complex where any relationship between that person and natural order and contours, between that person and any feeling of pleasure he might take in his work, is artificially induced—then he will lash out in frustration at the society that has diminished his humanity.

What we are witnessing today is an intense desire to return to the values of an integrated life based on human-scale proportions: a style of living that is life enhancing, not life negating, and that includes one's "work style."

In 1976 photographer Jeremiah O. Bragstad and I completed *Converted into Houses*, a book that told about places built originally as barns, ferryboats, firehouses, factories, railroad cars, and for other nonresidential purposes that had been converted for residential use. The owners were universally proud of their dwellings. They had been willing to commit time, money, and energy to these projects, and each and every one of them recited a litany of pleasurable factors about living in such warm, unusual spaces. Our conversations with them led to thinking about the places where people work.

We live in an era in which people are closely scrutinizing the type of work they are doing to support themselves. Consideration of the place where one works is a logical extension of this examination. For example, dentists, as a group, express great dissatisfaction with their work. One dentist who transformed a storefront located in a former brick warehouse into a Victorian-décor office recounts how this change in work atmosphere from a sterile space in a large medical-dental building created a different mental and emotional attitude toward his work.

The cheerful faces, low turnover, and enthusiasm for productivity at the industrial-design firm located in a restored ferryboat are probably the direct results of the unusual working space. Lunch can be eaten on a deck overlooking San Francisco Bay, and the atmosphere is more one of leisure than of toil.

The attorneys who have elected to house their offices in wooden Victorian mansions or in brownstones are opting for warm, comfortable, pleasing working spaces.

Those who saw the Oscar-winning film *The Apartment* will recall the opening scene: serried ranks of desks in a cavernous office. The desire to escape from the deadening uniformity and stultifying anonymity of such work spaces is motivating more and more people to experiment with transforming old establishments into comfortable new work places. Walls with texture, wooden floors, windows that open, high ceilings—these are but a few of the amenities they are seeking in their work environments. The experiments of some of these people are portrayed in the following pages.

Many older constructions, reasonably maintained, will last longer and prove more aesthetically pleasing than contemporary buildings. The restless demolition of buildings and their replacement by new construction that characterized Western Europe and the United States during the post–World War II years is now seen as having contributed to urban malaise by intensifying population and disturbing patterns of community life.

Was New York served by the demolition of numerous blocks of buildings, many of them dating from the early and mid-nineteenth century, and their replacement by the World Trade Center? Where would most workers prefer to spend their working hours—in a renovated, century-old, three-story brick building, or in a mammoth skyscraper?

There is yet another factor to consider when discussing the recycling of structures for unusual work spaces: conservation of resources. We have discovered in this decade that resources are limited. The waste of excellent space, materials, and money through automatic destruction of sturdy, serviceable older buildings is no longer looked upon as "progress." The new social climate of "lowered expectations," "zero growth," "human-scale surroundings," and "preservation of resources" is not amenable to tearing down buildings and entire sections of cities for vague reasons of "more space" or "more jobs."

Perhaps one of the best examples of this new social climate is Ghirardelli Square in San Francisco. A vast brick complex built in the late nineteenth century that housed, until the late 1950s, a chocolate factory, Ghirardelli Square was slated for demolition after the company moved into modern facilities. A huge apartment complex was planned for the site.

However, a wealthy, public-spirited San Franciscan, William Matson Roth, purchased the buildings, and over the next decade transformed the property into one of the most distinctive complexes of shops, offices, and restaurants in the United States. Not coincidentally, Ghirardelli Square is one of the most popular tourist attractions in the West.

It is not only the tourists and San Francisco shoppers who enjoy the historical patina and colorful grace of Ghirardelli Square. The men and women who work in its shops and offices are unanimous in voicing their pleasure at working in such unusual surroundings.

Are conversions of existing spaces prohibitively expensive? This question was asked constantly of

Jeremiah Bragstad and me after the publication of *Converted into Houses*. Our answer was to point out the range of possibilities as exhibited in the book: from conversions that cost but a few thousand dollars and were accomplished mainly by the owners themselves, to elaborate transformations that cost a great deal of money and called for the services of architects and contractors. The space itself, how much work an owner is willing or able to do, what the owner wants to accomplish—these factors go into an assessment of conversion cost.

In the pages that follow the cost range for converting unusual structures into working spaces is also evident. For some conversions elaborate design and construction work were desired or necessary. In other cases painting the walls of a loft space, staining the wooden floors, and adding an occasional partition and appropriate decoration converted a drab, empty space into an exciting place to work.

After questions about cost, the most frequently asked question is: Where do I find buildings that can be converted? The answer is quite simple: Everywhere. There is a virtually inexhaustible choice of structures that can provide unique working spaces. An elaborately designed bank built in the early twentieth century is abandoned after a merger; it becomes a record store. A gas station, closed because a new freeway has bypassed it, becomes a boutique. A ferryboat rotting in mud flats is rescued and used for an industrial design firm. The lofts of empty warehouses and industrial buildings—empty because industry and

warehousing have moved to industrial parks in suburbs—
provide some of the most common opportunities for
renovation.

Other possibilities are limited only by the fertility of
one's imagination. Obsolete ships, railroad cars, windmills,
abandoned firehouses, wineries, breweries, barns,
Victorian houses, and a huge variety of industrial buildings
are among the categories of structures that can be used as
working spaces.

It would be naïve to expect that the conversion of
unusual structures and obsolescent buildings will supply all
the working space that an industrial economy needs.
Obviously, large manufacturing facilities such as automobile
and aerospace plants cannot be accommodated to such
conversions. The proliferation of service businesses in the
United States and Western Europe, however, provides
numerous possibilities for such an approach. Professional
firms and small craft manufacturing facilities provide
others. And retail stores are yet another possibility.

This book is not intended to be a "how to" book. (I
would recommend the excellent handbook sponsored by the
Society for Industrial Archeology, *Working Spaces: The
Adaptive Use of Industrial Buildings*, as a beginning guide.)
Instead, *So This Is Where You Work!* is meant as a
photographic and textual sampling of what has been done.

I hope that this book will cause people to consider
the importance of providing similarly congenial working

environments. A defined need for persons to work in such environments instead of in the sterile, depersonalized office buildings and factories that are so much a part of industrial states might also inspire architects to design and build new buildings that will serve this need.

I wish to thank all those who recommended buildings for possible inclusion in this book, and those owners and operators of the buildings that have been included. Their cooperation and generosity were essential to the successful outcome of this project. And my gratitude, appreciation, and love to Sharon Allegra Moore, who could almost be considered a co-author of this book. Without her dedication, devotion, and belief in this endeavor, the book could not have been completed.

Charles A. Fracchia

## church/government offices

**T**he First Presbyterian Church of Novato, California, was built in 1896. Shipping magnate Captain Robert Dollar provided the lumber that was used for its construction, and William J. Steele, a trustee of the church, drew the plans and offered to supervise construction for $2.25 a day.

Sixty-seven years later, in 1963, a new church building was constructed and the original was sold to the city. Located in the downtown section of the newly incorporated city of Novato and close to the freeway off-ramp, the old church provided the ideal location and the perfect façade for the new city hall.

Consequently, the exterior of the church was kept intact, while the interior was partitioned for use as city offices. Some further renovation has taken place since 1963 to accommodate the growing needs of the community and the increase in the city staff.

As one city official put it, "I know it's funky, but this church has served our needs very well. And the price was right when we bought it." He did not comment on whether the structure helped in any way to keep city officials on "the straight and narrow."

church/government offices

### wedding chapel/retail shop

**T**he structure that now houses the Marmot Mountain Works, Ltd., in Berkeley, California, was built as a wedding chapel in 1929. In fact, it was *the* most popular wedding chapel in California during the 1940s, when burial services were also added to the program. So efficient was the transfer from one ceremony to another that floral décor and lighting could be changed within ten minutes!

Such prosperity ended in 1971, however, when noise emanating from nearby construction was so intense that at times the organ could not be heard. The chapel was forced to close.

The building remained vacant for five years before the partners of Marmot Mountain Works, Ltd.—a retail shop selling mountaineering, backpacking, and skiing equipment—decided that the Hansel and Gretel exterior of the former chapel, which resembles a Swiss mountain chalet, would make an excellent storefront for their merchandise.

## wedding chapel/retail shop

Since two of the Marmot partners are carpenters, the conversion was accomplished by them. The floor was refinished, wainscoting and cabinets were added, and a greenhouse effect was achieved by covering a portion of the ceiling with vines and adding side walls composed entirely of glass. The bottom portions of these walls contain stained-glass panes with floral designs; the upper windows are cut in arc shapes. What was once the organ loft now serves as office space. The exterior of the building remains the same, and even the chapel sign, proclaiming "Love Never Faileth," has been retained.

The Marmot partners have turned the foyer of the former chapel into a gallery in which the work of local photographers is exhibited.

## ELEGANT PROCEEDINGS
### Victorian homes/law offices

**M**ichael Kennedy and Joseph Rhine chose a ramshackle pair of Victorian flats in San Francisco to house their law practice—which specializes in radical political causes and drug cases and whose clients include Angela Davis and Timothy Leary.

Noticing that FBI operatives were photographing the building during remodeling, Kennedy and Rhine decided to twit them by painting the building a bright red (red remains the interior motif as well). "If they were going to accuse us of being 'reds,'" said Joseph Rhine, "we decided to give them good cause for doing so."

The building that Kennedy (who now practices in New York) and Rhine bought was constructed in the 1890s. By 1969, when they purchased it, it was in dilapidated condition, and they spent $10,000 to convert it. The distinctive Victorian decorative elements were preserved—and even augmented. Chandeliers, fireplaces, and liberal wood paneling were all retained, as well as stained-glass windows and elaborate plaster work on the walls (not shown).

A patio was constructed in the back yard, where, on sunny days, employees can eat lunch or enjoy a break from work.

## Victorian home/law offices

**I**t was certainly worth it," says Richard Moran, a partner in the law firm of Kutsko, Moran & Mullin, which in late 1974 bought one of the most impressive Victorian homes in San Francisco, and during the following year spent well over $100,000 to convert the building into law offices for the firm and for other attorneys to rent.

"It's made a great deal of economic sense for us," Moran continues. "We own the building, which has gone up in price, and we get income from the attorneys to whom we rent space. Over a period of time, the money we put into this building will be amortized, and we end up with a good investment and a spectacular place to practice law."

## Victorian home/law offices

The house was built in 1895 in the fashionable Pacific Heights section for Edward Coleman, a successful gold-mine owner. After his death in 1913 it was used successively as a club for card players, a boardinghouse, and, during the 1960s, a lodging house for "hippies."

Kutsko, Moran, and Mullin had all worked in downtown San Francisco office buildings before they purchased the Coleman mansion. "We were tired of the sterile environments in which we spent most of our waking hours," says Kutsko. "We wanted a place that was pleasing to work in," adds Mullin. The lawyers did not use an architect or general contractor for the conversion, but directed the work themselves.

Despite its six thousand square feet of space and its magnificent Queen Anne appearance, the shabby structure that the trio bought was in great need of repair. The roof needed replacing; the wood, staining; the interior and

exterior, painting; and the decorative features, restoring. Plastering, rewiring, and major plumbing repairs were also in order. The only reconstruction involved the kitchen of the former house, which was converted into the law library.

The attorneys were especially fortunate in knowing a niece of Edward Coleman who provided them with photographs of the house during its use in the late nineteenth and early twentieth centuries. The pictures enabled them to duplicate such features as the original chandeliers, Oriental rugs, and furniture.

The stained-glass windows, an outstanding feature of the mansion, were stolen just before the attorneys made their purchase but were recovered a few months later when a real-estate agent who had been assisting with the sale of the house discovered them in a local flea market.

Associates in the firm, secretaries, and clients alike praise the arrangement. For those who work in the building, the amenities make the hours far more pleasant than if they were laboring in a standard office building. Some even jog during lunch hours and are able to return and shower before resuming their afternoon duties.

## COUNTRY NEST EGGS . . .
### houses/banks

**T**he historic residence of Connecticut governor S. A. Foote and an 1811 farmhouse in Rocky Hill, New Jersey, have recently found new uses as banks—to the delight of residents of both communities who appreciate the preservation of these landmarks.

The Connecticut Savings Bank, in Cheshire, combined in its design philosophy a desire to restore the 1769 two-story, gable-roof structure and to implement the functional changes required for banking operations.

The original form of the building was kept. Interior partitions on the first floor were removed, although original materials were retained wherever possible. Only the fireplace, cased in paneling salvaged from the house, remains as a free-standing element. The interior of the building is decorated with many pieces of antique furniture, accessories, and artwork.

The site of the newly founded Montgomery National Bank was once on the path of a stagecoach route. The Bolmer House, as the structure is known, was left in its original condition, although the interior was extensively, but sensitively, remodeled for its new use. The original wood ceilings, the double-windowed entrance, and many other features of the former dwelling were retained.

## . . . AND A STABLE RETURN
### barn/antique shop

**T**om Kaye, a Yorkshireman and former farmer in Surrey, England, was delighted when he discovered that the 1867 barn he purchased for his antiques business had been built by another Yorkshireman—James Cudworth, a dairy rancher, who used the barn as a stable for his horses.

When Kaye purchased the building in 1965, he decided to preserve its original appearance. He painted the exterior red and white, left the beam ceilings exposed, and retained the original wooden floor, which now gently slopes.

Considering its former uses—as a first-aid station at the time of the 1906 San Francisco earthquake and fire, as a storage area for the booty of thieves and looters in the post-earthquake period, and as an upholstery shop—the barn has been remarkably well preserved.

# FIRE SALE
## firehouse/marketing group

**E**ngine Company No. 1—also known as the Phoenix Company—was the oldest of San Francisco's famed volunteer fire companies. The 1877 building that it originally occupied was destroyed in the 1906 earthquake and fire but was replaced, two years later, by a two-story sandstone structure with an Italian Renaissance façade and a keystone-arch entryway.

By the 1950s the building had become obsolete as a firehouse. The courtyard behind the building no longer served as a stable for the horses that had once pulled the steam-powered fire engine, and the turntable that had been used to turn the engine around (rather than backing it in) was no longer in use. A new firehouse was constructed, and the city sold the old home of Engine Company No. 1 as surplus property.

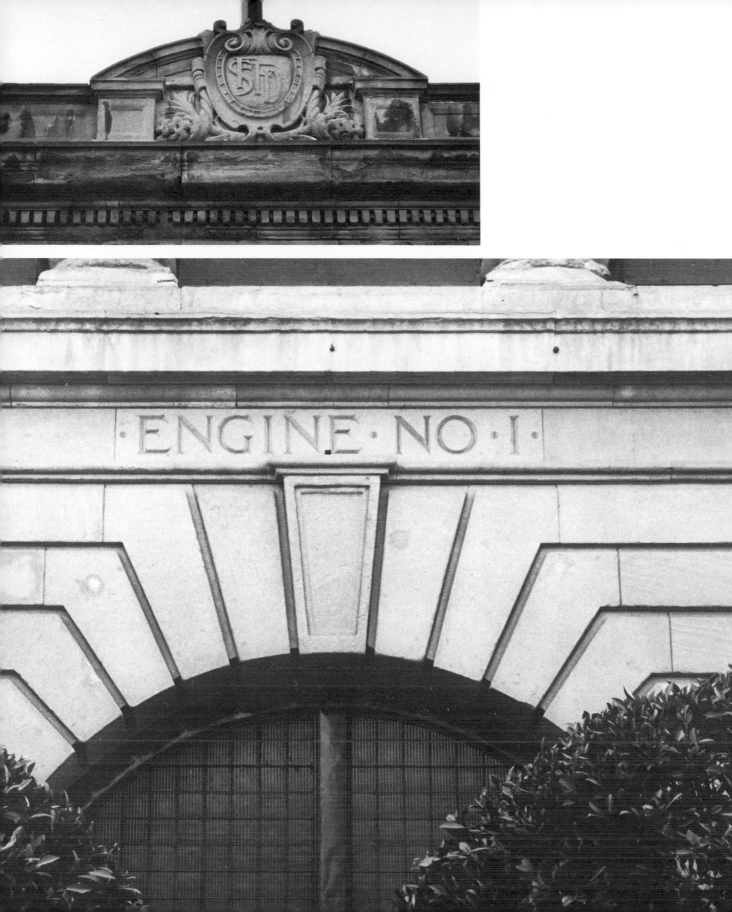

## firehouse/marketing group

Purchased in 1960 by Joseph Weiner, the building was made into three stories by lowering the ceiling of the second floor (originally living quarters for the firemen). Architect Lloyd Flood and landscape architect Thomas Church combined their talents to create a spectacular environment of elegant suites and a magnificent garden in the courtyard.

The brass firemen's pole remains in the building, together with a replica of the original circular iron staircase, and the red firehouse lanterns flanking the entryway continue their vigil.

Since 1973 the building has housed Ferguson-Hildreth, Inc., a marketing group that represents fifteen lines of contract furniture. The firm's interest in old buildings has spread beyond San Francisco: their Seattle office and showroom, The Ale House, is located in the refurbished hundred-year-old Ranier Brewing Company building.

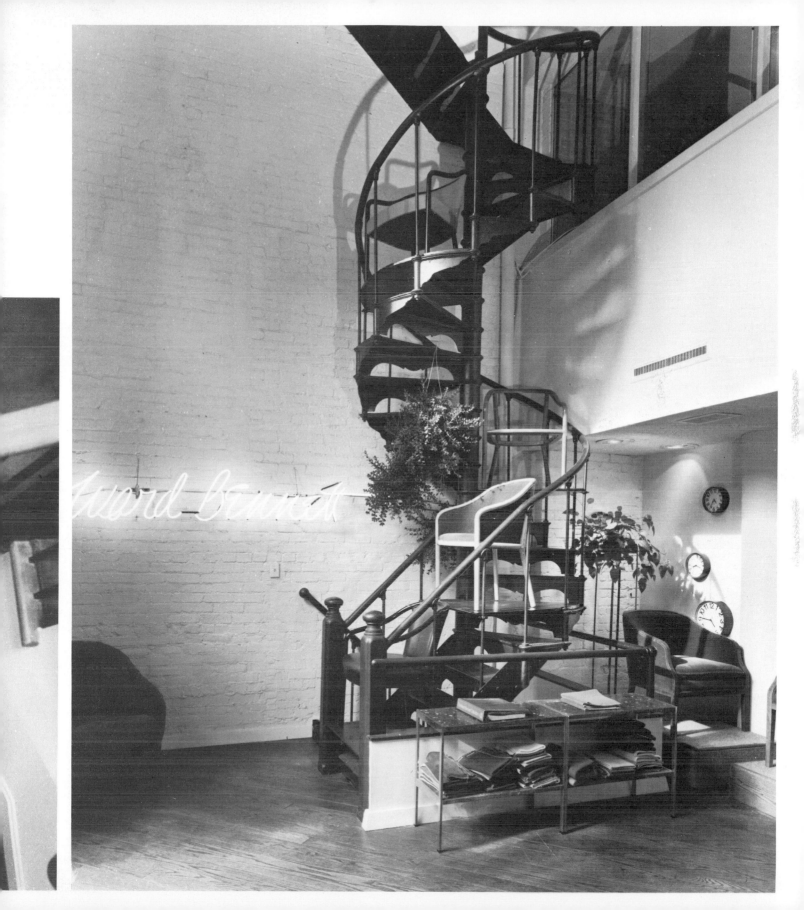

## firehouse/marketing group

# FIREHOUSE FARE
## firehouse/restaurant

**S**acramento was a bustling "jumping-off" point for prospectors during California's Gold Rush. In the early 1850s it became the state's capital, and in the 1860s it became the commencement point for the Central Pacific—the western portion of the first transcontinental railroad.

Much of the original city still exists and has been gradually restored as Old Sacramento—a section that utilizes renovated mid-nineteenth-century buildings for commercial purposes.

The restoration of these buildings was pioneered by the Cope family, who converted an 1853 firehouse into a restaurant, called, appropriately, the Firehouse.

The elegant two-story restaurant, with the legend "Sacramento No. 3" emblazoned across its façade, has an outdoor eating patio in what was once the firehouse's back yard. Here, sitting among sculpted trees and shrubs, one feels transported to the ambiance of an outdoor café in Europe.

The Firehouse is typical of mid-nineteenth-century western firehouse architecture, and despite its interim use as a storage warehouse the structure was in excellent condition when the Copes purchased it in 1960. Very little work had to be done for its conversion, and the restaurant's decorative features emphasize its firehouse origins.

### firehouse/restaurant

The conversion took a great deal of courage on the Copes' part. "The place was in the midst of one of the worst slums in California," says co-owner Carl Cope, "and it took some imagination to see the building's possibilities. And there was some initial fear that the area might scare off people." But the restaurant was an immediate success.

The volunteer fire companies in the West were established not only for fighting fires but also as social organizations similar to fraternal orders. Thus "Sacramento No. 3" used to ring with the merry sounds of numerous social occasions. Today those who lunch and dine at the Firehouse echo that bygone conviviality.

HOURS OF OPERATION
LUNCH MONDAY - FRIDAY    11:30 - 2:30
DINNER MONDAY                5:30 - 10:00
TUESDAY - THURSDAY    5:30 - 10:00
FRIDAY - SATURDAY      5:00 - 11:00
SUNDAY                        5:00 - 10:00
BRUNCH SATURDAY - SUNDAY 11:00 - 3:00

SANDWICH BAR
MONDAY - THURSDAY    11:00 - 4:00
FRIDAY - SUNDAY          11:00 - 4:00
BAR    MONDAY - THURSDAY   11:00 - 12:30
FRIDAY - SATURDAY      11:00 - 1:30
SUNDAY                        11:00 - 11:30

QUINN'S LIGHTHOUS

## LIGHTHOUSE REPASTS
lighthouse/restaurant

During their senior year three students at the Cornell University School of Hotel and Restaurant Administration agreed that they would open their own restaurant one day. They did better than that: Peter Lee, Bob Freeman, and Dick Bradley transformed their agreement at Cornell into a successful, publicly owned national chain of restaurants called Victoria Station (see also pages 56–57 and 68–69).

Although the majority of Victoria Station restaurants are converted railroad boxcars (decorated, appropriately, with historic British railroadiana), there are dramatic exceptions, including a 1903 lighthouse, located across the bay from San Francisco in Oakland, which the company opened in 1972 as Quinn's Lighthouse.

## lighthouse/restaurant

The lighthouse—it once guided ferryboats through storms and dense fogs between San Francisco and Oakland—was slated for demolition when Donald Durant stepped in and bought it for one dollar. It was transported to its present site by the world's largest water-borne crane, en route to Australia at the time.

lighthouse/restaurant

## DESIGNING ON ANOTHER PLANE
### catwalk/architectural office

The catwalk at Pier 1 on San Francisco's waterfront has a history of aborted uses. The pier was constructed in 1927 for use in the sugar trade, but was never used in that connection. During the 1930s it was turned over to passenger boats that plied the Sacramento River between San Francisco and Sacramento. The catwalk was to be used as a disembarkment area for passengers. Riverboat traffic soon ended, however, and, again, the catwalk served no purpose.

The space was subsequently abandoned, and in 1972, when Donald Danmeier, AIA, discovered the catwalk, it was being used by an inventor as storage space.

Danmeier and partner Barnabas Smith (later joined by architect Marshall Balf) leased the eight-foot-wide space and proceeded to convert it into an office. Among the reasons that impelled Danmeier and Smith to locate in the catwalk were the low rent, the excellent natural lighting, and the proximity to San Francisco's downtown retail and financial districts.

The two partners did all the reconstruction work themselves, working evenings and weekends for four months, and the total conversion cost was in the neighborhood of $2000. Notable features in the handsome office are a French oak door at the entrance, which was given to Danmeier and Smith by the owners of a turn-of-the-century house that was torn down for an apartment complex; and a wrought-iron garden gate with a decorative design of leaves, vines, and spirals, which now serves as the ground-floor entry to their offices.

## A CHARGED ATMOSPHERE
**power station/woodworking studio**

In 1896 the Pacific Gas and Electric Company, a fledgling combine that within the next few decades would become one of the largest utilities in the United States, established a stone power substation in the foothills of the Sierra Nevada mountains—in Nevada City, California, one of the principal mining towns of the Gold Rush.

The substation was eventually abandoned, and in 1972 was purchased and converted by Eben W. Haskell for use as his design and woodworking studio. Haskell added a deck and did some construction on the second floor; but the building still retains all the characteristics of its original use.

"I thought it would be a shame," says Haskell, "to let the building be torn down. It was perfect for my use, and cost me a lot less to buy and renovate than if I had leased or bought newer construction."

## RE-BERTH
**ferryboat/industrial-design firm**

The gentle roll of the ferryboat anchored to a pier on San Francisco's waterfront is definitely discernible. But it is the splendid office structure converted out of the ferry *Klamath*, built in 1924 to convey one thousand people and seventy-eight automobiles on each trip between San Francisco and Sausalito, that rivets one's attention.

After the *Klamath* was retired in 1956 it was purchased by a group who wished to turn it into a restaurant. These plans never materialized, and in 1964 the *Klamath* was sold for $12,000 to the world-renowned industrial-design firm of Walter Landor & Associates.

The ferryboat's bottom was sandblasted and sealed with a protective coating; electronic equipment was installed to deter corrosion. Decks were leveled, windows glazed, and a deckhouse—or mezzanine—was added for the Landor Museum of Packaging Antiquities, a collection of thousands of packages and memorabilia tracing the development of package design and technology. Partitions were put up, and ceilings lowered, but the original wood-exposed beam construction was retained. Natural woods—redwood and Douglas fir—were used for paneling in some of the offices. Lighting is of ferryboat vintage wherever possible. The original passenger stairway amidship was taken out and a grand staircase of natural wood leading from the main deck to the saloon deck was installed in the stern. In the bow the two decks were connected by a circular iron ladder. Total cost: $90,000.

### ferryboat/industrial-design firm

The elegant saloon deck is reached by walking up the staircase. A long corridor leads past design studios, beneath the retained smokestack, to the executive offices (Landor's is called the Captain's Cabin) and to a large conference room filled with the latest electronic gadgetry. All offices, studios, and research centers on both decks have inspiring views of the San Francisco skyline or of San Francisco Bay.

"The ferryboat is accessible to clients," says Landor, "and they love to come here. . . . Both our clients and the people who work here have a feeling that they're cut loose from the constraints of the city and from conventional thinking."

So unique, comfortable, and pleasant is the *Klamath* as a work environment that it enables Walter Landor & Associates to attract the best creative talent from throughout the country. There are even waiting lists of applicants for secretarial positions.

"But do you know what really makes this office complex unique?" asks Landor. "On July 2, 1944, a U.S. Navy submarine crossed the *Klamath*'s bow and was rammed. That makes this the only office building in the world to ram a submarine."

## GROUND TO TASTE
### feed mill/shops and restaurants

Petaluma, California, was once known as "the chicken capital of the world." So important and profitable was its production of poultry and eggs that by 1915 more dollars per capita were on deposit in Petaluma banks than in any other city in the United States. This prosperity ended, however, in the early 1950s when the price of eggs came crashing down.

The oldest building in Petaluma was constructed by the town's founder, Thomas Bayliss, in 1854. Once a warehouse and a feed mill, it was called the Golden Eagle Milling Company and stood from 1854 to 1964 as a monument to the thriving agricultural base of Petaluma. By 1975, however, it, along with some adjacent historical buildings, was slated for demolition.

## feed mill/shops and restaurants

Wishing to preserve this historic heritage and sensing that a conversion of the mill and the other buildings would be economically beneficial, real-estate man Skip Sommer purchased the property, obtained the necessary authorization, and converted the buildings to new uses.

The Great Petaluma Mill was completed in 1976. (Earlier Sommer had successfully converted, among other structures, a Victorian residence and a gas station.) Some thirty-three retail shops and restaurants are now housed in its twenty-eight thousand square feet of space. The businesses are extremely successful, and the project has drawn wide attention and approbation.

"In each of the conversions we saved a historic building due for demolition," says Sommer. "Public response has been excellent. Those who work in the buildings enjoy the environments in which they spend their time; and the people who come here to shop and dine are extremely happy with the places."

Sommer had some advice for those who are contemplating the conversion of obsolete industrial buildings, particularly if they are historic. "I'm sure that anyone interested in converting an old building will find that first he will have to prove himself to very skeptical public bodies. A good approach is to start with the local historical or heritage societies. Once you have them on your side, you have added power at city hall. But nothing can beat the 'before and after' pictures of something you've already done."

## grain-milling plant/corporate headquarters

**E**ven the corporate headquarters of Victoria Station is a unique conversion (see also pages 44–48 and 56–57). The San Francisco building was originally Globe Mills, a grain-milling plant built in the 1880s. In addition to the converted mill, and in keeping with Victoria Station's railroad motif, real-estate developer Ron Kaufman, who specializes in adapting old buildings to new uses, has transformed the observation car from the "Flying Scotsman" into a conference room. The car stands at one side of the building's entrance, the site of the former loading dock.

The interior of the building features open-space planning using fabric panels. A London taxi rests in the middle of the floor. The thirty-foot ceiling is skylighted, and a balcony surrounds the work space. Off to one side is a gymnasium and saunas for the employees, as well as a test kitchen—all of which were adapted from space already existing in the old mill building.

# A PACKAGE DEAL
## cannery/shops, offices, restaurant

An imposing early-nineteenth-century Del Monte cannery in Marysville, California, was successfully converted into a delightful complex of shops, offices, and restaurant in 1964. Under the leadership of Jack Gavin, a group of Marysville investors created 520 Olive, as the complex is known, in a move to prevent Montgomery Ward, a major retail store, from leaving the city. The store was subsequently located at one end of the building. Other offices include an architectural firm, an insurance company, and a law firm.

The massive brick structure contains many of the interior features that were part of its original construction: wooden beams, skylights, and exposed brick walls.

"It's been a recycling process," says Dan Desmond, whose interior-design firm occupies space in the cannery. "The city has saved a major retail concern; and the reconstruction has brought new businesses into the area, provided hundreds of jobs, and created a splendidly attractive place for people to work."

### winery/shops, offices, restaurants

In 1870 the newly constructed Groezinger Winery in Yountville, California, took part in the state's pioneering attempt to produce quality wines in the Napa Valley. As the years went on, production became more and more successful, and now millions of visitors trek annually to this premium wine-growing area to visit the numerous wineries in operation.

The Groezinger Winery, however, no longer attracts visitors who wish to see a working winery. A number of years ago what was once the largest winery in the Napa Valley was considered inefficient by modern standards and was relegated to stabling horses.

Today's visitors to the Napa Valley generally *don't* pass up the chance to stop at the old Groezinger Winery, now renamed Vintage 1870. In 1967 the large brick building was converted into a shopping complex: some thirty antique, art, craft, clothing, wine, and food shops, as well as two restaurants and a summer theater, combine to create the atmosphere of a restrained bazaar.

## winery/shops, offices, restaurants

Aside from its attraction for local shoppers, tourists, and a regular clientele from the San Francisco Bay area, Vintage 1870 has also become a much sought after location for professional offices. Those whose offices are located here express their delight in working in a rustic setting.

A great deal of interior reconstruction was necessary for the conversion. Lofts, staircases, and other features had to be built, but so great was the owner's concern for keeping as much of the old building intact as possible that, for instance, the building's façade and the old floor planking were retained.

# CAST IN BLUEPRINTS
## coppersmithery/architectural offices

**H**oward A. Friedman's architectural firm was located above an onion warehouse on San Francisco's waterfront for twenty years. When the wind blew in a certain direction, the watery eyes of Friedman and his staff attested to the pungency of the commodity stored beneath their offices.

In time the office space proved too small for Friedman's business. In fact, the only compensation was a dramatic view of San Francisco Bay and the Golden Gate Bridge.

Then came an eviction notice: the building was going to be torn down. In 1973 Friedman bought a coppersmith's factory (built in 1922), and converted it the following year.

"It was something I had always wanted to do," says Friedman, whose only concession to his former location was to reproduce photographically the view of San Francisco Bay and hang the photograph in its mock window frame in the bathroom of the firm's new quarters.

He retained as many reminders as he could of the building's use as a copper manufactory: the exterior still bears the name of its previous owner, E. M. O'Donnell Copper Works; the extravagant floor-to-ceiling height (E. M. O'Donnell manufactured huge fire-protection systems for ships) has not been cut, but alleviated by a minimum of partitions that create several individual offices; large orange cranes (which had to be screwed to rails), chain doors originally used for loading, as well as other appurtenances, have been left about, and smaller artifacts have been hung on wooden pillars or walls.

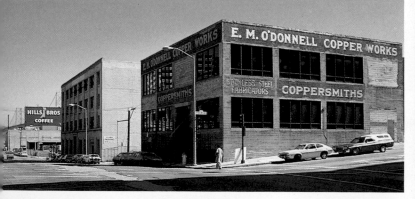

Exposed wooden ceilings, white reinforced concrete walls, and dark wooden floors combine to convey warmth and a pleasing visual pattern in the cavernous space. In addition, a color spectrum covering part of a clerestory window throws a rainbow into the interior of the building when the sun is shining.

Abundant plants, in addition to the space and the light, make the interior of this architectural firm as pleasing to the eye as any exterior view.

## automobile repair shop/architectural offices

**D**onald Sandy, Jr., AIA, and James A. Babcock, architects and planners, exercised a heroic feat of imagination when they decided to convert an automobile body repair shop in San Francisco to offices for their firm.

The cavernous, grimy building, which was built in 1863, challenged the skills of the two partners and their associates, who undertook its transformation into a spacious, light, airy, handsome working environment.

The walls had to be made earthquake-proof, as required by the building code, and the existing building had to be reinforced, which accounted for a substantial portion of the renovation costs. A functioning office environment had to be created within the interior space.

The results are spectacular enough to have won the firm an Award of Excellence in Renovation and Preservation in the second annual National Design and Environment Awards Program.

The entry-room floors are of black slate. Just off the entry is the managing architect's office. A pulley door, bare brick exterior walls, and white interior walls give this office an aspect of the building's former use.

The entry room leads to small conference rooms, and to a complex of open-work cubicles and a kitchen area.

In the midst of this main floor is an interior patio containing plants and trees. Light comes from an overhead skylight. The contrast of exposed wood, iron, and bricks and the pleasant horticultural complex mitigates the strong impression of the building materials.

Iron spiral staircases lead up to two mezzanine platforms: the rear mezzanine containing the firm's library and a subsidiary interior-design firm; the front mezzanine containing a conference room, two enclosed offices, and some open office space. Looking down onto the main floor, one feels as if one is in an aerie.

### automobile repair shop/architectural offices

The employees of Sandy & Babcock are unanimous in expressing their pleasure at working in this environment. "The feeling of space and light makes working here quite pleasant," says one. "You don't feel like you've been thrown into four walls and a floor and ceiling, and told, 'Here's where you're going to be spending the major portion of your day.' You relate to this environment as much as you do to a home environment you like."

## A PALATABLE SOLUTION
### Chinese laundry/restaurant

An 1891 building in San Jose, California, served as a Chinese laundry for many years. In 1955 one side of the building became an auto repair garage, and twenty years later the entire building was converted into a restaurant.

Removal of old "ovens" in the building yielded 20,000 bricks—and provided the restaurant with additional space. The interior of the building was gutted and the old timber was used to reinforce the structure. The original skylights, the brick walls, and the façade, however, were retained.

The Laundry Works Restaurant, as it is known, offers dining in a delightful garden-patio atmosphere. Amid trees and plants and nineteenth-century charm, patrons can enjoy a visually exciting ambiance.

84

## LOFTY BEGINNINGS
### feather factory/architectural offices

For fifty-four years chicken feathers were cleaned and fluffed in a building near San Francisco's waterfront. The operation required a large, lofty space in which huge vats for feather-washing and stairs, catwalks, and decks for overseeing the vats could be located. By 1965 the feather business was on the decline and the building was put up for sale. Architect Donald Knorr decided to convert the 1911 factory into offices for his firm and for other tenants as well.

Knorr made the most of the great volume of space at the center of the top floor and of the unusual system of stairs. According to his designs, a stairway was built and an elevator was installed to service the entire building. It took about six months in all to remove many of the floor drains and steam tanks, sandblast the original roof rafters (which were retained), and paint the interior entirely white. But the extraordinary result is a source of pride for all who work in the building.

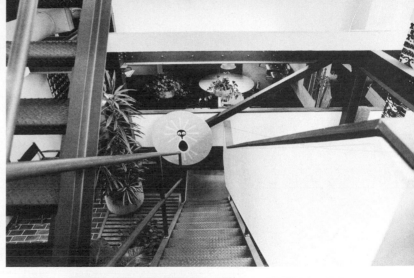

### renovated clothing factory

**I**n 1906 a company that had originated during California Gold Rush days constructed a three-story wooden factory to replace the facilities it had just lost in the San Francisco earthquake and fire. The company, Levi Strauss, is world renowned for having revolutionized the clothing industry.

By 1970 the building was no longer an efficient manufacturing facility. Company officials considered replacing it with a new factory, but many of the employees, who were attached to the old building and believed that it contributed aesthetically to the neighborhood, persuaded Levi Strauss to retain it.

Architect Howard Friedman renovated the factory and added four outside stairways to provide more interior floor space. To enhance the neighborhood further, he added a playground in front of the building.

One of Levi Strauss's almost one hundred worldwide manufacturing facilities, this factory specializes in men's corduroy jeans, and the building is a self-contained unit for this production: patternmaking and shipping departments are located on the first floor, manufacturing on the second, and design, product research, and production departments, as well as research laboratories, on the third.

### commercial building/clothing boutique

**T**he origins of the nineteenth-century commercial building in Chicago that now houses the Ann Taylor boutique have been lost "in the mists of time." Before its conversion in 1976 the building served as an art gallery, but little is known beyond that.

Extensive renovation was carried out to convert the building into an elegant retail establishment: the interior was gutted, six steel beams were added to support a mezzanine; modern air-conditioning, heating, and fixtures were installed, and a new façade was built.

Despite these changes, however, Ann Taylor retains the distinctive flavor of a nineteenth-century industrial building. Skylights in the rear of the ceiling-vault roof, a circular wooden stairway, and two-story display windows combine to convey a modern effect tinged with antique elegance.

**paper products, whiskey warehouse/shops, offices, restaurants**

**B**ricks salvaged from the 1906 San Francisco earthquake and fire provided the building material for many new structures, including a large six-story warehouse that served a national paper products firm and then, after Prohibition, became a storage place for whiskey. An unusual feature of the 1907 warehouse was the interior courtyard that was used as a loading dock for trucks.

It is this central courtyard that provided a focus for the warehouse, the conversion of which resulted in one of the most unusual shop and office complexes in the country. The building was purchased by Walter Landor and Joseph Weiner in the 1960s, and the principal architect for the conversion was Lloyd Flood.

An Irish pub, a flower stand, and a shopping arcade surround the courtyard. Iron railings, an effective and aesthetic way to disguise necessary fire escapes, cascade down the walls of the courtyard. Large gas lamps are a handsome addition to the luxurious red-bricked enclosed area, and other turn-of-the-century motifs are used by many of the commercial establishments in the building, notably by the bank.

paper products,
whiskey warehouse/
shops, offices,
restaurants

### spice factory/dental office

I t was something Dr. Bruce Marcucci had always wanted to do: get out of the usual space in which most dentists practice. His search for an unusual environment brought him to an old spice factory, built in 1907, which had seen subsequent use as a wholesale warehouse and as an import/export business.

Marcucci obtained a favorable long-term lease for the ground floor of the building and proceeded to convert it into an unusual dentist's office with the help of architect William Weber Kirsch.

Workmen found the building easy to work with as they turned the one thousand feet of space into an open area in accordance with Marcucci's vision of how he wanted to practice dentistry. The brick walls and wood beams were sandblasted and left exposed. A back and side wall were added, as well as an oak floor.

Rather than divide the space into rooms, low partitions were used to preserve an openness for both offices and areas where dental work is done. A profusion of plants, Oriental rugs on the dark-stained floors, and exquisite antique dental furniture give Marcucci's office—shared with partner Paul Hoyt—color, warmth, and intimacy, and relieve the immense openness.

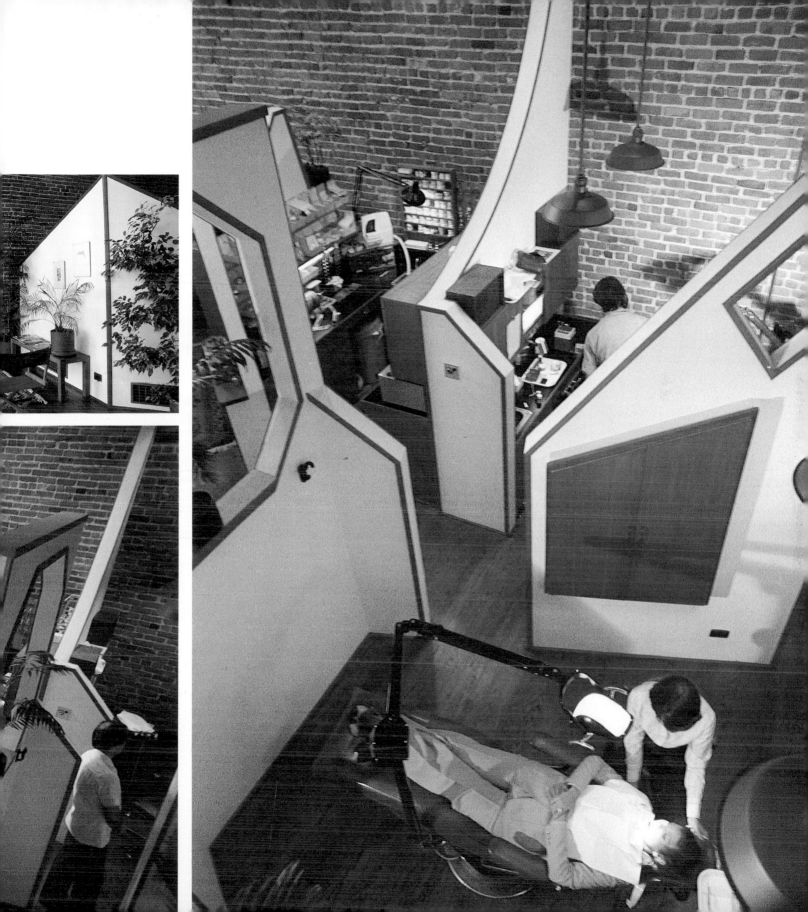

### spice factory/dental office

"Our patients love this office," says Marcucci. "They can look into the place from the street, walk right into the reception area, and have work done in an open, casual, and pleasant atmosphere. They can bring in their own tapes, put on earphones, and listen to whatever music they like. I like working here, Paul likes it, the people who work for us like it, and our patients—as much as anyone can like going to a dentist's office—like it."

Marcucci, who claims to be a frustrated architect, believes that "people should put their money where their mouths are." He justifies his spending $30,000 to convert his office by stating that it is beneficial to both him and his patients. The cost, he says, amortized over his twenty-year lease, is not excessive for the result: probably one of the most pleasant dentist's offices in the country.

## stables/law offices

**T**he building in which the law offices of Landels, Ripley & Diamond are located has had an unusual past. Since its construction in 1906, it has served as stables (for horses that pulled fire engines from a firehouse that was located across the street); as a bordello; as a cigar factory; and as a warehouse until 1972, when it was extensively remodeled for the ill-fated move of the *Saturday Review* to San Francisco.

At that time all interior partitions were removed from the three-story brick building and a new steel frame was added (to make the building earthquake-resistant).

Offices cluster around what is essentially one central open space but which is in effect a series of spaces that are open either up to the roof or down to the level below, providing an intricate and always-changing spatial experience. None of the openings, however, extend the full height of the building, although from the reception area there is a view up through the building to the skylighted roof.

The bare brick walls, the brightly painted air ducts, and the sandblasted wooden support pillars and ceiling beams combine to give the offices of Landels, Ripley & Diamond a contemporary appearance and a traditional feeling.

**stables/law offices**

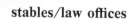

## CONSUMERS' CHOICE
**supermarket/shops, offices, restaurant**

The Franchini family of San Anselmo, California, were pioneers when, in 1926, they established Home Market, one of the first supermarkets in the United States. As the store specialized in meat and fish, it was not surprising that developer Skip Sommer, who acquired the abandoned building in 1973, chose to call the new development the Butcher Shop. The building now contains twelve boutiques and a restaurant on the ground floor, and six offices on the second floor.

Not one to lose a built-in opportunity for a dramatic display of a building's former use, Sommer has retained the old Home Market's meat racks, which are now used by the boutiques to display merchandise.

## A LEARNED POLICY
**life insurance company/college and "consciousness" organization**

The earthquake and fire in San Francisco destroyed sixty percent of the city. Among the companies whose buildings—and records—perished was the Metropolitan Life Insurance Company. Metropolitan Life took no chances in constructing its new headquarters three years later, in 1909. Designed in the classic Ionic style, with a touch of French Renaissance, the new building was built to withstand an earthquake of up to 8.5 magnitude on the Richter scale.

Structural steel and reinforced concrete were used in the building's construction. The façade is of terra cotta veneer, the interior is marble, and the door and window frames in many parts of the structure are brass. The ceilings on the fifth floor are decorated in gold leaf, some in Greek and French borders, others in all-over French patterns.

## life insurance company/college and "consciousness" organization

In 1973, when the Metropolitan Life Insurance Company moved its offices into a new thirty-eight-story high-rise, the fate of its former headquarters was in question. The site was up for sale for a considerable period of time, and fear mounted that the valuable property might be sold to someone who would demolish the exquisite structure.

In a daring move Cogswell College, an engineering and technical school, came to the rescue in 1974 when it purchased the property and transferred its educational facilities there. The move provided Cogswell College not only with one of the most elegant campuses imaginable, but also proximity to San Francisco's financial and business community. Other tenants, principally *est,* the international growth movement organization, took space in the building.

For *est,* the move represented a consolidation of the spread-out offices of this successful "new consciousness" organization. The Barry Brukoff–designed interiors are vivid, exhilarating, yet quietly conducive, and, with living greenery lacing every vista, evocative of nature. A festive banner-hung ceiling greets one's upward glance.

Although no training is available at the new headquarters, a large number of visitors, trainers, staff, and volunteers, working day and night, need a warm, efficient space to carry on the organization's multiple activities in a flexible manner.

For the students, teachers, and staff of Cogswell College, for the *est* staff, and for the other tenants in the building, a large interior courtyard serves as a pleasant oasis in the midst of a complex of high-rises, and the panoramic view of San Francisco from the roof provides a visual treat.

## SURPRISES IN STORE
### warehouse/shops and restaurants

**T**he conversion of nineteenth-century industrial buildings for contemporary use has yielded structures that preserve beautifully the distinctive architectural style of those monuments to the advance of the Industrial Revolution in the United States. Industrial architecture became less substantial and less distinctive during the twentieth century, however, when this massive Chicago warehouse was built. But a group of developers recognized the merits of transforming the bleak structure into a complex of shops and restaurants, and the results—a farrago of color and contemporary lines—are quite dazzling. Exposed brick walls are offset by lush hanging plants; a sense of openness was created by cutting away parts of floors and by the use of balconies; window enlargements produce a cheerful, light atmosphere.

According to the developers, it would have been economically unfeasible to have created a similar complex by new construction. The sense of mass, the plentitude of materials, and the opulent space—all of which contribute to making this converted warehouse into a pleasant, profitable, and successful shopping center—would be impossible to duplicate today.

ALL OF THE ABOVE

### warehouse/advertising agency

**I**n 1968 Dancer Fitzgerald Sample, Inc., a national advertising agency, needed more office space. A warehouse, built in 1907 along San Francisco's waterfront, was found, and after it was pronounced sound, a building committee selected from among the company employees studied the problems of converting the structure into a new home for the agency.

Two principal design problems had to be solved: first, the arrangement of necessary work spaces on the second floor that would preserve everyone's view of the existing timber trusses; and second, an entrance and main stairway that would draw visitors to the second floor from the street with as little effort and as much drama as possible.

Starting with straightforward loft space, the Dancer Fitzgerald Sample building committee and the architects for the conversion decided that most of the private offices would be located around the perimeter. All the offices are roofless so that the structure above can be seen. The inviting entrance, visible through the arched façade from the street, focuses on a reception desk that is halfway to the second floor. Views up to the vaulted space from that point tie the two parts of the design firmly together.

## warehouse/advertising agency

The interior space combines sufficient offices, conference rooms, and studios—all on one floor—with a sense of quiet intimacy. The sloping office walls follow causeways that give the appearance of a maze. The austere white stucco offices contrast effectively with the rich red-brick outer walls.

# A SHOWCASE FOR REEL ESTATE
## movie theater/shops, offices, restaurants

**C**hicago's Century Theater was built during the years 1922–1924. Like most movie palaces of the 1920s and 1930s, the Century, an ornate, four-thousand-seat vaudeville and movie theater, became obsolete.

Unlike many of its contemporaries, though, the Century had a prime location near three arterial streets in one of the city's most densely populated areas. It was this advantage that prompted Selwyn Malisoff, president of E & S Realty, to develop the theater into a shopping complex—a most dazzling complex at that.

Malisoff's first move was to turn to Jerome Brown & Associates, a design firm experienced in residential and commercial renovations. Brown gutted the old structure and created an essentially new self-supporting structure within the old bearing walls of the theater. "All we were left with were the shell and the gallery that led to the balcony in the old theater," says Brown. "We kept the shell and the ornate terra cotta façade as mementos of another time and another way of life."

### movie theater/shops, offices, restaurants

During its construction the Century (the name given to the development) fell victim to spiraling construction costs. As a result, builders and designers tried to economize where they could, without sacrificing the quality of the materials used.

Visitors entering the building pass by curved-glass display windows and walk beneath a ceiling of polished stainless-steel cubes. The entryway directs them to the building elevators or invites them to walk around the ground level. In the center of the structure is an open eighty-foot-high central court, accented by a skylight and an exposed elevator shaft.

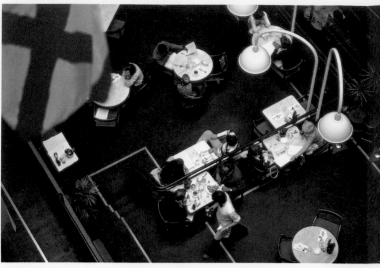

**movie theater/shops, offices, restaurants**

In following the spiral of ramps, topped in black concrete, down from the top level, shoppers pass virtually every shop and restaurant (which number more than sixty). At the base of the spiral, in the central court, is a café, and additional tenants—including a miniature golf course—are found in the basement.

The extraordinary building, which intimates its former gilded interior splendor, draws a large segment of the community not only for shopping but also for weekend activities.